William "Bill" Carlson
An Autobiography

William "Bill" Carlson
An Autobiography

with Daniel J. Vance
Foreword by Glen Taylor

©1999 by AdVance Creative. All rights reserved.

AdVance Creative
P.O. Box 154
Vernon Center, MN 56090

Photos for chapters one through fifteen provided by William Carlson.
Photos for cover and chapter sixteen by Kris Kathmann.

Designed by Kris Kathmann.

ISBN 0-9672014-0-3

Foreword

Bill Carlson put his life in God's hands. It appears his business plan came straight from the Bible, and it shows in how he treated everyone, his employees, customers and family. Bill has the greatest integrity. He was respectful of everyone at all times, honest to a fault and willing to share his knowledge and good fortunes with others. He didn't take advantage of people or situations. By constantly following these basic beliefs, he attracted customers and employees who were loyal to him. This allowed Bill to build a strong company foundation that today, over fifty years later, still has his hand prints on every part of it.

Our relationship was very special. Many people assumed we were related or that I was his son-in-law. Not so. Yet, in many ways he was like a father to me. Though neither of us showed our emotions outwardly, I could feel and see his love and pride in his eyes and actions. I had similar feelings for Bill. He was the mentor I needed, and I respected his guidance and judgment. He was conservative and experienced. I was the student who learned from the teacher by following his example.

– Glen Taylor
May, 1999

Age 4.

Chapter One

Grief washed over me as the train pulled out of town. The only family that had ever loved me was back at the station, waving, while I gripped the armrest with white knuckles and tried holding it in. But I couldn't hold it in forever. The anguish was far too much. Tears began flowing down my cheek and onto the armrest. The train towards Oregon was gaining speed. With each chug, chug, chug, of the steam engine, the lump in my throat grew larger and larger. Minnesota would soon be a distant memory. I looked at my reflection in the window and watched my lower lip tremble. I began sobbing and a woman tried to comfort me. My heart was being torn apart and there was nothing I could do. But I had to obey my dad.

Surely they could have warned me, a ten-year-old, that they'd be taking me away. After three years my dad and his new wife were swooping in out of the blue and stealing me from Aunt Hannah and Uncle Lorens. Dad spoke almost apologetically when he said I had to go with him to Oregon, like he knew he would be hurting me by doing it. And while he spoke, my new step-mother seemed almost rude, shifting her weight from one foot to the other, like she wanted to get on with it.

"I guess you'll have to go," said Aunt Hannah, her gentle hands massaging the back of my neck, but her touch didn't comfort. Uncle Lorens stood alongside with his head bowed, gazing at his feet. I wanted this to be just a bad dream. "But I don't have to go," I said before biting down on my lip. "I want to stay here with you." Aunt Hannah squeezed my neck like she wanted to keep me with her.

Dad touched my shoulder with his rough farmer's hand. "C'mon," he said with a forced smile, "you'll like it there. It's a big town, lotsa boys. You'll fit right in." But I didn't fit in. Oregon wouldn't be the same as Minnesota.

Most boys live with just one family before their tenth birthday. I lived with five families. The instability of my early years, and the years beyond, shaped and molded me into the person I am today. But to better fill you in on the type of person that founded Carlson Craft, perhaps I should take you back to the very beginning and tell you everything along the way.

My paternal grandparents, Anders and Anna Carlson, emigrated to the U.S. in 1882 from Sweden after poor economic times. They had been potato farmers. In the U.S. they farmed in Illinois first, then moved to southwestern Minnesota near Slayton. There they helped found Bethany Lutheran Church where Anders was an active Lutheran and deacon. My grandmother soon became a Baptist after feeling out of place with the Lutherans. Many of them were much better off financially than her. She wanted to be nearer people in her own social class. So Grandmother raised eight of the children, including the youngest, Harry, my dad, as Baptists, while Grandfather raised the oldest son, John, as a Lutheran. In later years, Grandfather did worship with the Baptists, and he's buried at their cemetery alongside Grandma.

Like my grandmother in the 1880s, I feel very uncomfortable when people make distinctions along class lines.

I was born February 26, 1915, at Balaton, Minnesota, a town that today straddles US Highway 14. It's twenty miles from Slayton, and not that far from either South Dakota or Iowa. Sadness struck me early in life. I was three when Grandfather Carlson died, four when my mother died of tuberculosis, and five when Grandmother Carlson died. If she were alive, I'm sure my mother would be proud of me today. I have a picture of her holding me in her arms right before she died, and I've often wondered what went through her mind when that picture was being taken. She certainly knew then that she would die. Tuberculosis was a dreaded disease back then. It must have been upsetting her that she wouldn't be around for her only child.

She died at home, and I was not taken to the funeral. The casket sat near the front window. Afterwards they burned her clothes outside the house to destroy the tuberculosis germs that they thought were in the clothing.

I've often thought about my dad and how he had to rebuild his life from scratch. In 1918, he lost his father, in 1919, his wife, and in 1920, his mother. Add to that his failure at farming in 1922 and it nearly did him in. His failure at farming really wasn't his fault, but caused by a farm depression that affected every farmer in the early '20s. After my dad suffered through these four major catastrophes in four years, he became rather passive in business and in life. One blessing: He didn't seem to suffer any long-term depression and lived to be ninety-three.

After Mom died, Dad bought a farm in North Dakota and left me behind with my maternal grandparents, Andrew and Johanna Nelson, who had also immigrated from Sweden. They first settled in Michigan, after which they bought a farm near Slayton. Johanna was a dedicated Christian and farmer's wife. They worshipped at the Swedish Baptist church north of Slayton. School was two miles away, quite a walk even for a farm boy. Early on I learned from the Nelsons that my mother had wanted me to be a "William" instead of a "Bill." When the other kids found that out they began taunting me over and over again by saying, "Bill, Bill." I answered them by saying: "My name is William Dewey Carlson, not Bill." A neighbor kid stuck up for me. Even today I sign my name William 'Bill' Carlson, but only because so many people call me Bill that it has to be noted.

The Nelsons gave me two rabbits as pets. That Easter I went out to the barn and found Easter eggs where the rabbits normally slept. To this day I don't know how they got there. Don't rabbits lay eggs?

After two years with the Nelsons, Dad wrote for me to join him in Merricourt, North Dakota. The train trip from Slayton across the bland prairie seemed so desolate and treeless and lonely for a six-year-old. During my eighteen months in North Dakota, I never once attended school, church, or played with a child my age. Frigid winter winds reaching thirty below would knife down from Canada and cut right to the bone. Dad farmed with his brother, Art, and two hired hands, and they all treated me well. They grew wheat and farmed with horses. The land agent who sold Dad the land had exaggerated its value. I visited the land a few years ago, and it seemed like good farm land, but Dad had paid far too much for it. Combine paying too much along with the farm recession and what little equity he had in the land didn't warrant holding onto it. After he lost it, he never again bought another farm.

There wasn't much for a young boy to do on the prairie. An old plow originally made for a steam tractor fascinated me, and I would play with Dad's canceled checks and pretend they were real money. He would have wanted them to be real.

After losing the farm, he sent me to live with his sister, Hannah, and her husband, Lorens Larson, while he found work as a hired hand in southern Minnesota. The Larson's farm was on the other end of the state, in northwestern Minnesota, and hundreds of miles away. Even though this was the second time I'd been left behind, I didn't feel as abandoned as I could have by Dad because the Larsons filled the gap with love almost immediately. By then I was seven, and their son, Clarence, was eight. Another son, Leonard, was twelve, and Mabel, eighteen. They worshipped at a Covenant Church, where I began to wonder why I couldn't take communion along with everyone else. School was a mile away where Melva Mickelson, my teacher, encouraged me scholastically. She skipped me over fourth grade into fifth even though I had started school late in life, and her encouragement, especially in geography and history, helped me appreciate those subjects later on.

Several events stand out as shaping my character at this time. One afternoon after school, like most boys, I had the idea that to be 'grown up' I had to have a smoke. I found some dried weed by the road and nearly died from it. It wasn't tobacco. I'm glad I smoked it because it sure cured me of wanting a cigarette. Then another time, with Clarence, we found a nozzle from a fire engine in a ditch. A fire at a neighboring farm the previous winter had burned a barn near there. After returning it to the fire department, we earned a ten dollar reward, which Clarence and I split 50-50. Honesty rewarded can impress a young mind.

We didn't have Nintendo. When radio arrived in 1924, I listened in at a neighbor's house. Our games were simple. We played Pump Pump Pull Away, Red Light, Hide and Seek, and Tug-O-War. Rubber tires from an old car became a pretend car, and we "drove" them down the road by rolling them along by hand. A metal rim from a wagon with a stick jammed in the hole served the same purpose. I didn't have a single toy car or fire engine, which would have been incredible toys, because my aunt and uncle couldn't afford them. They couldn't even afford a bicycle, even though most children had one. My first bike ride didn't come until I was fifty-nine. I haven't fallen off yet.

The Larsons lived near Crookston, Minnesota, a wheat-growing area in the Red River Valley. Their farm was tiny compared to the one Dad had owned briefly in North Dakota. Lorens farmed his 160 acres with horses, and hauled wheat seven miles to a grain elevator. Crookston had an old-fashioned grocery store that bought rhubarb from my aunt and uncle for resale. This exposed me to selling wholesale. I helped feed chickens and hogs, and pick eggs, but was too young to milk the cows. It was honest work. When the chores were done at 9:00 at night I'd eat Hannah's homemade bread, which she made in the afternoons too. If you haven't tasted homemade bread, you've really missed something!

Aunt Hannah was loving and kind, and her many praises held me up when I was down. She became a real mother and I felt warmed by her love.

At ten, after three wonderful years, my world was turned on end once again when in February 1925, Dad and an unfamiliar woman showed up on the Larson's doorstep. They said they were taking me with them to Oregon, but I didn't want to leave the only family I'd known. "But you have to go," Dad said. The new woman, he added, was my new step-mother, Emily. So now after ten years I would be joining my fifth different family unit. As the train pulled out of Crookston, the Larsons waved and cried, and I wouldn't see them again for twenty years.

My father and step-mother.

CHAPTER TWO

It hurt leaving the family I loved. My cries soon tapered off to whimpers as the prairie train chugged towards North Dakota and on towards Oregon. No one understood my pain, I thought, and I felt all alone in the world. I tried to push the Larsons out of my mind and focus on the scenery that swept by the window, but time again I kept returning to them and breaking down once again. Who was this woman who said she was my mother? What if she died like my real mother?

The city of Powers, with a population of 2,000, was a logging community in western Oregon at the very end of the railroad line near the Pacific Ocean. It was two thousand miles from Minnesota, which made it seem like the other side of nowhere. My dad managed a ranch for a vice president of a lumber company and earned $100 a month, which was a lot then. Nearly all of my new relatives were connected to the lumber industry. For a few weeks we lived in an apartment before moving into the only two-story building in town. We didn't have much money: Breakfast, day in and day out, consisted of toast with elderberry jelly but without butter, and milk poured over oatmeal. My folks didn't own a car, and neither did my grandparents.

The passenger train that puffed into Powers every day became my entertainment for a while. The engine stayed overnight in the roundhouse, and chugged out under steam power in the morning. This scene took place outside my bedroom window every morning, and sometimes while watching I'd dream about taking it back to Minnesota.

Everything about Powers scared me. The lumberjacks drank, gambled and fought, and their children were my school classmates. My step-grandfather was a communist and he read the Milwaukee Journal, which espoused radical views. His wife wore the family pants, and regulated and manipulated nearly everything. Once she erected a six-foot fence between her house and her neighbor's because she hated them so much. The Ku Klux Klan burned crosses on a hillside overlooking the Coquille River, and it was the only time I've ever had an experience with the Ku Klux Klan – and hopefully my last.

I had a surly attitude with my step-mother that first year. One day I sassed back to her and she had Dad spank me, something which hurt my heart more than my behind.

Social contacts revolved around my grandparent's house, where my parents would show off my new step-sister, who was born our second year there. Emily was too high-strung to be a mother, and I challenged her authority every single step of the way. She had never raised a child before, and now was stuck with a snotty ten-year-old who wasn't hers, and a newborn.

In school I was an average student, and given my internal makeup, I could have excelled if someone had pushed and encouraged, but no one did – though I yearned for someone who would.

I've visited Powers three times since the 1920s, and for some reason I keep going back, like the swallows to Capistrano. Perhaps I've been searching for meaning in a period of my life that didn't have any. If we'd stayed my life would probably have taken a turn for the worse. The only explanation for why I survived is that God must have been there through it all. Then at the end of three years in Oregon, my parents decided to move home to Minnesota. It was a miracle for me.

Guste and Christ.

CHAPTER THREE

Minnesota was where my best memories took me. Immediately upon arriving in Balaton on March 1, 1928, my parents arranged for me to live with a Mrs. Sylvia Morgan, my step-mother's sister, in order to finish out the school year in town. I didn't mind, because I wouldn't have to live with my step-mother out on the farm. Every day, I hitched a ride with a neighbor to eighth grade in Balaton.

Curious, I visited my maternal grandparents, who had raised me for two years very early in my life, and I soon discovered that a lot had transpired since. My grandfather was alive, but my grandmother had died about the time we'd left for Oregon. Her obituary said that at her advanced age of sixty-five, "it had not been advisable" for them to try and revive her. This makes me chuckle because at this writing I'm nearly twenty years older than that "advanced age."

After a summer spent working on a farm where my dad was a hired hand, I was told I'd be staying in Balaton for my freshman year that fall with an Aunt Augusta and Uncle Christ, relatives of my step-mother. "Guste" and her husband turned out to be excellent role models. She was like her mother in Oregon who ran the family, but Guste differed in that she never flaunted power or manipulated others. Uncle Christ was a family man, good businessman, and perfect gentleman. My parent's occasional donations of eggs and meat didn't even begin to cover the cost of my food, clothes and housing, but it didn't matter because with their soft hearts, Guste and Christ would have taken me in for free anyway. I became the big brother to their two little daughters, Maxine and Marion.

Christ was an International Harvester farm implements dealer in Balaton, and had a thriving business until the farm economy, and then his dealership, failed in 1933. He'd sold too much farm equipment on credit and been far too lenient with his customers. Many farmers could not or would not pay him, and right as his cash flow tightened, International Harvester squeezed him. Even when some farmers were making headway again in the late '30s, not one paid him their old bills. I learned from his experience. Despite the painful memories of Christ losing his implements dealership, I have always thought well of International Harvester, and it remains my favorite tractor.

Then more sadness hit. The original agreement between Guste and my parents was to be good for only one year, after which I was to attend a rural school and live with my parents. And that's exactly what happened. Now I was being torn away from a loving family for the second time. That September, I walked or rode horseback to school eight miles a day round-trip, and it didn't take a rocket scientist to figure I'd freeze making the trip in January. In addition, the rural school didn't have the quality or quantity of teachers in Balaton. So one day I rode into town and knocked on Guste's door, and emptied my soul to her. I told her I wouldn't be able to walk to school in January, and that she'd have to take me back. As she sat listening and nodding her head, I could tell my pleas were reaching sympathetic ears. I ended up staying with her throughout the rest of high school.

Finally, somebody was pushing me to do well in school. When I had homework, which was nearly every night, Guste made certain I did it. She was pulling every little bit of potential I had right out of me, and in that respect she was like Hannah. The void I had felt in my heart for Hannah was quickly being filled with the love Guste was pouring in. She was a loving housewife, mother, church worker, and she mixed well socially – probably because her husband was a businessman. Though short of stature, like Hannah and myself, Guste worked extremely hard and I began to pick up her work ethic. I don't remember anyone ever saying anything negative about her.

Through her influence I attended, and became a member of the Methodist Church in Balaton. This was the first time I'd been exposed to church or Sunday school. I was baptized at fifteen, in 1930. The Methodists didn't believe especially in sudden individual conversions – salvation was a gradual process for them, and that was my experience. After hearing the Gospel I came to the belief that I should accept Christ and be baptized. The Epworth League was its youth group, and we would travel to other towns and meet with their youth groups. At one such meeting at Tracy, Minnesota, I heard the hymn "Have Thine Own Way, Lord," and it instantly became my favorite because it helped me make sense out of life. I realized then that my mother's death, my dad's farming failure, the years with Hannah, unhappiness in Oregon, nurturing with Guste – in all these God was having His own way with me. God does mold and make us.

The Epworth League was definitely instrumental in my decision to accept Jesus Christ as Savior and Lord. Over a six-year period there two different pastors suggested I go into the ministry after high school. I learned a special scripture verse there, too: "I can do all things through Christ who strengthens me." Remembering it has helped me endure tough times, and it can help you too.

God worked through Guste's life in a silent, but consistent way. Methodists then, and she was one, didn't express much excitement over their salvation. It wasn't lightning bolts and Damascus Road for her or me, but I did experience a definite turning point in my life. This decision for Jesus Christ instantly ignited a desire in my heart to read the Bible and try to understand it to the best of my ability. I read it through almost immediately and have continued reading it to this day. In fact, I have the same New Testament Rev. R. J. Wilson gave me senior year, in which he'd scribbled, "William Carlson, you are your master, you alone can keep yourself from doing what you wish." My son-in-law, an Evangelical Covenant pastor, has taken issue over that wording, but I think in my case it helped more than hurt. My son-in-law says it tells me to rely on my own strength and not on God. In my eyes, Rev. Wilson was simply urging me to improve on what God had given me.

Accepting Jesus Christ and Guste's nurturing transformed me into an excellent student almost overnight. My first two years at Balaton I'd been average. During my junior and senior years I worked harder, and eventually became class valedictorian. Eldora Olson was my chief "rival" in grades, and her mere presence urged me on. I worked hard to "beat" her and become valedictorian. My senior year I topped the honor roll. I received the Citizenship Award, which was an all-around medal for student activities and the first awarded in Balaton High School history.

Superintendent Almen wrote me this note of encouragement: "William you are a very fine young man. Fellows like you make me feel that education is worthwhile and can keep Democracy safe." Superintendent Almen's statement boosted my confidence even higher, and it helped me do my best – with God's help, of course. I'm not sure how much he knew of my background, and how much I needed his encouraging word, but what he said really hit fertile ground.

Just because I'd become a Christian didn't mean I was perfect. I still had rough edges. In history class a teacher asked about the voting record of the German Reichstag on a particular issue, and I answered, "three-hundred ten to two ninety-eight," without raising my hand. She didn't like the fact I'd spoken without raising my hand, especially after one of my buddies started laughing his head off at me. The teacher threatened to throw my friend out the window. My buddy learned not to laugh at a teacher, but more importantly, I learned details aren't that important sometimes.

My senior year our basketball team made the state tournament and the script played out like the movie, Hoosiers, in which a rural school makes it to the state championship game and wins. Well, it wasn't quite like Hoosiers. We lost the first game, but at least we made the trip. Today a banner in the school's gymnasium memorializes '32 as the only Balaton High team ever to reach state, and I was part of it all as team manager. Our school had only forty boys, and the entire senior class had but eighteen students. Our great coach helped build the team, but he couldn't shoot or pass. I learned that good leadership and a dedicated squad can accomplish almost anything, and the same can be said for business.

Winning or losing was a fraction of what we learned under Coach Earl Olson and Supt. Almen. They pushed each player to do his best. The summer before that school year, knowing the team had potential, Supt. Almen had sent a letter to each player asking them to watch their diet, get plenty of bed rest, and build stamina before fall.

To help pay for the tournament trip, Balaton merchants took up a collection so we'd have spending money. That raised two dollars apiece. To raise more, the team hosted a chain of banquets, and people around town cooked special dinners for us. For Balaton, a trip to the state basketball tournament was as big as it got. Some team members have since said I was important in helping them win. What they said was nice, but overblown. My most significant contribution, besides mothering the basketballs and towels, was plotting the plays. If a player launched a basket from a particular spot, I'd mark in a notebook where it had been taken, and who shot it.

My small size and lack of athletic talent was a blessing in disguise. Since I didn't possess the physical attributes needed for most sports, I simply turned my competitive drive towards scholastic achievement. Surely God knew what He was doing.

Me and Fern.

Chapter Four

Every summer I endured staying with my parents at their farm near Balaton. It was obvious they favored my half-sister, Fern, over me. They would always fill her school lunch pail with fruit, which was a luxury item then, but never mine. Fern didn't have many chores, and that spoiled her. All this doting on her didn't settle well with me, and actually hurt quite a bit. All summer long I thought and dreamed about attending high school in the fall and staying with Aunt Guste.

    I worked until dark every day, went to bed, woke up, and worked until dark again. The routine seemed like it would never end. On Sundays, my parents would visit relatives some twenty-five miles away and leave the chores to me. Of course, Fern went with them. Sunday chores consisted of washing the dishes and the cream separator, milking the cows and feeding chickens. I don't think Fern ever milked a cow.

    It ate at me. A cousin, an inventive man, built a glider and a real airplane one summer, but I never saw him or it because I had those Sunday chores. Later, when my mother died, I inherited one dollar from her estate. When my dad was alive, he had told me his estate would eventually be divided evenly between Fern and me, but my step-mother changed it all in her will. Losing the money didn't hurt; I'd been slighted.

    Even though I graduated in '32 and had a partial scholarship to Hamline University, I still didn't have enough money to pay for college. I wasn't alone in being short of cash. Superintendent Almen made arrangements with the University of Minnesota to establish a satellite school in Balaton where ten students enrolled in a one-year program to keep us interested until we could afford college. The program helped. We had the same classes U of M freshman had. I stayed with Guste while taking these courses.

    With the discouragement of not being able to afford college, and being worked to the bone, I lived for relief on Saturday nights in Balaton. I'd find a way there somehow. Saturday night farmers caught up on all the news from the area, Washington and St. Paul. Most arrived about 7:30 at night and socialized until 9:00, when they began their weekly grocery shopping. I'd watch a movie, visit other boys, or buy an ice cream cone.

I'd also buy these multi-flavored candies that looked like Lifesavers. Each time I'd finish emptying a load while threshing grain, I'd pop a candy into my mouth as a reward for a job well done. Later, in the early '50s, when we had the business in our home, I would walk to the post office every evening to send out mail. Afterwards I'd pop a candy into my mouth.

The summers of '33 through '35, I worked for Dad. At the time, his brother, Hjalmer Carlson, was a county commissioner and could have placed me with the Civilian Conservation Corps. He wanted to, but Dad said he couldn't afford to lose me. The people who took part in CCC earned $25 a month, and $20 of it had to be sent home. My dad should have said he couldn't afford not to send me, but perhaps he didn't understand the program.

Trying to save cash for college, I raised squash and sold sweet corn to restaurants in Balaton. In a way, it was my first wholesale business. The restaurants bought my corn at ten cents a dozen and sold it for fifty. It seemed to me like they were making money hand over fist, but of course I didn't factor in their rent, insurance and utility costs. Every year I'd sell over a hundred boxes of Christmas cards. I bought at fifty cents a box, and sold at a dollar. Spending money had to be earned because my dad never gave out an allowance.

Frustrated at times, I often felt like bypassing college and starting a career right away. I mused about becoming a baker because the bakery window displays always looked so attractive. Balaton had two bakeries, so one day I stopped by one of them to learn more. I asked the baker what training was necessary and he ended my aspirations immediately. "First, I get up every morning about two-thirty to mix the dough," he said. That ended that. Then I wanted to be a postal clerk, which seemed like a secure job, but for some reason I never followed through with the idea.

Me and Vi.

Chapter Five

My high school class had prophesied that I would be "most likely to succeed in business." A high school course had interested me in buying and selling. With my short stature, I wasn't cut out for the physical demands of farming, and besides, farming required long hours and a hefty financial investment. When considering where I might go for more education, I leaned towards a business college, which would cost less than a university and take less time.

Three schools sent me catalogs: Nettleton Business College of Sioux Falls, Minneapolis Business College, and Mankato Commercial College. I believed then that a catalog was a good indicator of the quality of the school. So I chose Mankato Commercial College because its catalog was the most attractive. Later on I applied this lesson learned with Carlson Craft when I emphasized catalog quality to grab the interest of the bride.

The fall before leaving for Mankato I picked nearly two thousand bushels of corn by hand, which netted me $100. In January '36, my last month on the farm, I worked for a farmer who paid $10 a month plus room and board. I had $130 for college.

As the train pulled into Mankato, in early spring 1936, I said to myself, "Mankato here I come." That may seem like a strange thing to say, but I said it anyway. I didn't have any reason to think I'd later own a large printing company. Entering business college was a major turning point in life, and I was about to make the most of it.

Outside of Minneapolis, Mankato, with 15,000 people, was the biggest town I'd ever seen. The presence of Good Counsel Academy, Mankato Teachers College, and Mankato Commercial College made it the educational hub of south-central Minnesota. Mankato Commercial College offered accounting, and all its classes were individualized and self-paced. I studied hard that spring before leaving for Balaton once again, and by the end of summer and flush with more cash, I was looking forward to coming back.

Because of financial needs that fall I worked right away. I spent $90 the first day on tuition, which left me $40. I found a dish washing job at a nice restaurant and worked there a "lifetime" – ten days. I worked thirty hours the first week and didn't receive a dime, just room and board. They wouldn't even let me eat menu food, just plain food. I realized then that there were many other students who needed a good part-time job while attending college as well.

Then I heard about an elderly widow who needed a helper. I paid Mrs. Schultz one dollar a week and helped her wash floors, clean, vacuum, and dust, and in return, she let me drive her car. On weekends I drove her to a sister in Vernon Center. She was young enough at heart to realize I needed a social environment, so she let me host parties at her home.

That fall I voted for Roosevelt, who had guided the country through the banking crisis. FDR had instituted the WPA, which was a program that helped put people to work. Formerly unemployed people felt useful again, and it wasn't done by just handing out money. Many people criticized it as "We Putter Around," but it was needed then. In my mind, Roosevelt, and later Eisenhower, were the greatest presidents in my lifetime.

Near St. Valentine's Day 1937, I met Viola Stoneberg, a farmer's daughter from Slayton, which was some twenty miles from Balaton. We'd never heard of each other before then. She was attending Mankato Teachers College. Vi and I rode back and forth on the train or bus together from Mankato to our respective homes in western Minnesota. She was beautiful. I'd have a hard time not staring.

April 1937 a job opportunity opened up at the Mankato regional office for National Refining Company, an oil company that competed with Standard Oil. I won a bookkeeping job over three other applicants because I could type. In the interview they had pressed me for my typing speed, but I couldn't answer because I'd never taken a test. I'd taught myself at the college during lunch hour.

National Refining Co., of Cleveland, Ohio, had good products and service, but not much vision. Standard Oil was eating it alive. The Mankato regional office ran seven filling stations and my job was billing. The gasoline came from an Oklahoma refinery where the base price was three cents a gallon. After adding freight and taxes in Mankato, the retail price for regular gas was about 19 cents.

Along with work and this young woman, Vi, who began taking hold of my heart, I was the spark plug for creating the Commercial College Gang, which was made up mostly of Mankato Commercial College students. We played around at local parks, had wiener roasts, told jokes. The group has continued to the present, and those of us left meet annually.

Vi and I differed in one major area: even though she would have to pay them back, her parents were still financing her education. She didn't have to work, and even lived in the dormitory. A two-year course was all rural teachers needed. Our relationship grew and in early May 1938, she rode a bus just to visit me in Mankato, and we spent the weekend together. Apparently she had cared enough about me to make the long trip. By then she was finished with school and was making her own money. We started going steady that weekend and my heart would race each time we talked. Vi was beautiful, slender, not tall, and she had many of the personal attributes I wanted in a wife: she was a Christian, beautiful, friendly. There wasn't anything about her I considered a negative. One trait, in particular, that attracted me was how secure she acted, something that must have sprung from her stable background. My background had been exactly the opposite. She was my first love, and I bought a used 1932 Chevrolet in December 1938 to drive out every month to visit her at her parent's farm near Chandler.

On the business side of life, the competition simply beat us. National Refining Company downsized on February 1, 1940, and had to move me and an office secretary to Dubuque, Iowa. Our office manager went to Kansas City, and seven workers lost jobs in the shuffle. Dubuque was lonely because Vi wasn't there. I missed my Mankato church as well, and tried to fight my way out of the loneliness by visiting a small Baptist church nearby, but it wasn't the same because the faces and names were different. Even though my job was a very responsible position that made me feel good about work, more so than my job in Mankato, National Refinery was losing money and I could sense trouble.

A friend, Wilber Holst, brought Vi down over Easter break. She tried on the diamond ring I gave her, but I wouldn't let her keep it because the timing wasn't right. That weekend we saw Gone With The Wind for the very first time, and the touch of her hand in the dark theater sent tingles up my spine. The movie characters became us. The night after she left I couldn't sleep. My mind whirled with thoughts that took me up into the clouds. I was going to be married. I was so convinced of it that I visited a pastor at a

Lutheran church in Dubuque and began taking adult religion classes. I even joined.

On June 22, 1940, I drove to Balaton, and officially proposed with my gentlest plea as the diamond ring rested in my palm. She said Yes. Dreams were becoming reality right before my eyes. A woman so wonderful had agreed to spend her life alongside mine forever. I had a great career and now a woman would be my wife. What could stop me now? We set the date for 1942 and talked into the night, but the next day, before I left for Dubuque, she seemed to change. What was happening? The glitter of the diamond in her eyes had dimmed. She said she didn't feel comfortable wearing it because her mother wouldn't approve. On the long and lonely drive back to Dubuque I didn't know what to think.

In a few months the Dubuque office closed, and the former office manager from Mankato asked me down to Kansas City. What I really wanted was a job near Vi. But without another job, I had to accept his offer. August in Kansas City was hotter than a firecracker. The National Refinery Co. office sat near the railroad tracks and livestock noises and smells rolled by day and night, and heat billowed off the tracks in thick waves that smothered and choked. And then they downgraded my responsibilities, which shot my morale. They had me running an adding machine all day and Vi was in Slayton and I missed her. When Curtis called just six weeks into this Kansas City grind, I was ready to go.

Curtis Brooks, my best friend from the Methodist Church in Mankato, was also first sergeant of a Minnesota National Guard unit that had just received orders to train for one year in southern California. War clouds were forming over Europe and the United States was readying many Guard units, like Curtis' 215th Anti-Aircraft regiment. I could type, so that qualified me to be his battery clerk. By joining up with him I could complete my one-year training in southern California, which seemed a much friendlier locale than England or France. Sooner or later Uncle Sam would call, I figured, so why not sooner but under my terms?

Anxious about Vi and seizing the opportunity, I returned to Mankato in October 1940. Curtis waived Guard summer camp for me because he said I was along solely for my typing skills anyway, not my marching skills. The Minnesota National Guard is supposed to help with only such things as domestic disturbances and floods in the state, but the federal government realized the Army was understaffed, and with war in Europe, had to build up quickly. Our unit would be in the first two percent of National Guard units sent overseas.

In Alaska.

CHAPTER SIX

Our unit was inducted into federal service January 6, 1941. We left by train for California as I waved good-bye to friends through the window glass. While the train slowly chugged away, I thoroughly expected to return, soothe Vi's fears about marriage, and live happily ever after. She'd seemed so distant when we'd parted at Slayton a few days earlier. A woman couldn't be married and teach at the same time in Minnesota. If we were to marry upon my return, she would have to quit and we'd have to live on my salary alone. A marriage could be kept secret, and some were, but that wasn't our style.

At basic training in Riverside, California, I opted out of field training because they needed me in the office. I was like Radar O'Reilly from M.A.S.H. In July 1941 our outfit was ordered outside the U.S., to Kodiak Island in the territory of Alaska, and no one in the unit had ever been there. After the Japanese attack on Pearl Harbor of December 7, I realized we wouldn't be home in Minnesota anytime soon. The nearby naval base and its submarines needed protection from Japanese aircraft, and we were ordered to move our office to a field position, and camouflage it and a bunkhouse. Kodiak seemed vulnerable because only one other outpost stood between us and Tokyo. False alarms and alerts erupted periodically. Alaska was not as boring as I had originally envisioned it to be.

Our commanding officer, Col. Frazer, 215th Coast Artillery, was a tough, regular Army officer who breathed and ate discipline. Even though Kodiak Island was rugged and frigid, any direct conflict with the Japanese seemed unlikely. He had chosen Alaska for our assignment, and he had chosen correctly. Guard units from northern Minnesota were nearly wiped out in the Philippines at Corrigedor. In 1982 I visited a charred barracks there and gave God thanks that I hadn't been with one of those units.

After awhile some men, including Curtis Brooks, moved out for officer training. When they returned, I couldn't associate with him or the others. He said "servicemen can't socialize with officers" and his attitude really grated at me. Now my best friend couldn't even talk to me! It wore me down and hurt deeply, and Alaska became a much lonelier place.

The colonel made me the official photographer for our ninety man unit. I snapped pictures and developed black and white photos at night in the mess hall. Censorship rules had to be followed. Along the way I was promoted from battery clerk to battalion sergeant major, and apparently I'd entered at the right time for advancement: with my typing experience, I'd started as a corporal, something highly unusual.

The entrepreneurial bug bit and I began selling Christmas cards again. I'd take the orders, deliver and collect the cash. I had nothing to hold onto now but Vi, and I was saving up extra money for the day she'd leave teaching and we'd marry. An official Army cloth shoulder patch made me more cash. The Army was slow in making them and demand began building. One time an officer left on emergency furlough, and on the way back he stopped at a Seattle clothing store that stocked these shoulder patches. When he arrived back at Kodiak, other officers wanted them, so I ordered twenty-five, and then five hundred. At the five hundred bracket, I could buy at twenty-five cents and sell for fifty. One time a mail ship was torpedoed, and some of the patches came in waterlogged. I made $750 off those patches, which was a lot compared to my beginning Army pay of about $7.50 a week.

Being thousands of miles apart, my relationship with Vi was unraveling. Even before I'd left I could sense her drifting further and further away. Now she was slowly ending our relationship in her letters. I felt so helpless on Kodiak Island with no way to see her or talk to her. I had no one to share my pain with but God. Curtis couldn't talk with me. Why was she doing this? In one letter she hinted at another man.

In a desperate move to win her back, for her birthday in September 1942, I had one dozen red roses sent to the school where she taught, and I also had a Kate Smith song called "One Dozen Red Roses" dedicated to her on the radio. You can't imagine how difficult it was to have radio station, WNAX, in Yankton, accept my song request from Alaska, which wasn't even part of the United States at the time. They feared a subversive effort. Was it secret code to a Japanese spy? Vi received the roses, but never heard the song. Her landlady had heard it, though. The roses and song ended up as parting gifts, and losing her was harder to accept than I realized at the time.

Shortly after my arrival in Alaska, the Christian Church in Mankato had started a letter program to encourage its servicemen and Helen Sherman became my penpal. I enjoyed her letters, especially after Curtis and I stopped talking, but after awhile she stopped and gave her duty over to a Betty Hoffman. She and I quickly developed a relationship by mail, and her letters were the salve that helped begin the healing process after losing Viola.

Later I learned that Vi's mother had talked her out of marrying me. She had wanted Vi to marry a farmer.

Betty and Me.

CHAPTER SEVEN

Through 1943, Betty Hoffman's letters were frequent. I had no idea when we started that we'd become more than penpals. At first we knew only of each other's names, and that we both shared the same church, but soon a romance developed. When I came home on furlough in February 1944, I presented her with flowers for Easter and that opened the emotional floodgates for both of us. During that same furlough I saw Vi and she returned the ring, which helped cut the emotional ties with her. Four months later, Betty and I were engaged. It was the case where my heart was still hurting and she filled the void quite nicely.

Betty was an extrovert. Where I internalized my feelings, she would say what she felt. She had taken typing and business training in high school – skills that would become very valuable when we began business later on. Betty was the only child of her adopting parents. She thought she knew her birth mother, but her parents never discussed that with her. Howard, her father, was a garage mechanic, and a hard-working, God-fearing man, and as an elder at the Christian Church he prayed some of the best prayers anyone has ever heard.

Herman Kooy, our pastor at the Christian Church, was from the Church of Christ and Minnesota Bible College. He was quite a man of God and very instrumental in my spiritual growth and in that of others. Over his pastoral career, which spanned sixty years, nearly one hundred and fifteen young persons decided to enter full-time Christian service while under his pastoring. That boggles my mind. I professed Christ as Lord and Savior at Mankato Church of Christ in June 1939, and it was Herman Kooy who baptized me.

After furlough in Mankato, I returned to Fort Bliss, near El Paso, Texas, but only for a short while. The Army renamed us the 599th Coast Artillery (AA). It sure was great to be on American soil and not in Alaska. Betty's parents were very protective by nature, so it amazed me when they let her visit Fort Bliss just three months after we had announced our engagement. We could have married then, but I didn't believe in marrying and marching off into war.

The Army sent us to England in December 1944 on the Queen Mary, which is now a Long Beach tourist attraction. It held 15,000 soldiers, and was built for 3,000. The trip took five days because the ship had to zigzag to evade German submarines. A couple of years ago, while at its Long Beach Visitors Center, I learned that the Queen Mary often had an American destroyer escort while making trips across the Atlantic during the war. One time an enemy submarine surprised it, and the Queen Mary's captain had to make a fast decision whether to zigzag or sail straight. By zigzagging he'd plow into a destroyer, but by sailing straight he would surely be sunk. Since the ship contained fifteen thousand men and the destroyer only three hundred, the captain zigzagged. For all I know, this could have happened on my trip over.

In the middle of an English winter, I caught pneumonia in an unheated barracks and it drained the life right out of me. We were northwest of London about seventy miles at an anti-aircraft facility that was a stopping off point before entering the European Theater. Because of the sickness, for a while it looked like I wouldn't have to fight the Germans. When our unit left for the continent, I was halfway through a nine-day stay in the hospital. Once recovered, I tried to rejoin them. But in the last weeks of the war, fuel and material had priority, so I had to be patient in catching up with my outfit. When I could finally start towards them, I caught pneumonia again in northern France. After recovering once again, I crossed the Rhine River into Germany at 11:00 A.M. on May 11, still a bit sick. When I finally reached my outfit, near the Danube, the river was not blue like the song, but murky.

The war was dying down. On July 5, my outfit completed its assignment and headed towards America without me. The Army assigned me to another unit because I had entered the battle zone too late because of the pneumonia. Army "battle points" determined which soldiers went home and which stayed. The very hour before I was to leave for my new outfit though, I discovered a special order that said anyone who had "crossed the Rhine River by midnight May 11, 1945, was entitled to his battle star."

I showed my new commanding officer the orders, and received permission to borrow a driver for a trip to Army headquarters in Nuremberg. I held on tight to those special orders. By crossing the Rhine River on May 11, my battle points were now at ninety-three, the lowest total anyone could earn and still go home. I stayed with my new outfit two weeks before boarding a train for Marseilles. From there I flew to South America, and later to Miami, where I celebrated VJ Day with the rest of the city. Miami had a ticker tape parade. I called Betty, and she was celebrating from her work at the Draft Board. A train took me to southern Wisconsin, and I was discharged August 20.

When I'd entered the Guard, the assignment was for one year. It lasted fifty-six months, and the good part of that without furlough. The Army stole a part of my life, and I had to defer marriage like many other men. But on the positive side, I was able to serve my country and gain valuable business experience along the way. I wasn't bitter. My Army experience taught me patience and perseverance.

Me and Betty on our wedding day.

Chapter Eight

Returning from the War I had $5,000 in my bank account, which was far more than what most soldiers had. I hadn't gambled like most nor spent that much on a girlfriend. My overseas assignment had earned premium pay. And I'd sold seventeen hundred boxes of Christmas cards, which netted $850 one year, and I'd made another $750 off the shoulder patches.

After a few weeks back in Mankato, I started with Truth Tool Company, a firm that made wrench sets and tools for customers like Montgomery Ward. The owner was not the best person to work under because she often would rake her employees over the coals. After the girl next to me was harshly criticized in front of coworkers, I decided my turn would be next. So I resigned.

Swanson's Wallpaper and Paint was next, a retail store, where I worked under a Christian man who gave me a great deal of work freedom. He let me be my own boss as the bookkeeper and contract figurer. The biggest benefit I gleaned from working there proved to be what I learned from their internal printing business that made paint labels and stationary. One day I happened to pick up *Graphic Arts Monthly* magazine, and read an article entitled "Profits with Printed Paper Napkins." It intrigued me.

Betty and I were married September 15, 1946. A year later, in September 1947, she was diagnosed with Hodgkin's disease. Our doctor immediately recommended a Mayo Clinic or Minneapolis lung specialist. One of her lungs was partially collapsed, and gurgling with fluid. We chose a Dr. Kinsella in Minneapolis because Betty had relatives nearby, and I knew a minister who would call on her. While taking her up there, I was quietly fearing that she would die. Of course, I didn't share that fear with her. Maybe she was fearing the same thing. She could hardly breathe and I winced each time she took a breath.

While Betty was at St. Mary's Hospital, I continued on at Swanson's. It was hard to work during the day when my wife was struggling without my support some ninety miles away. I drove up on weekends and every other night in what was a four-hour round-trip. During the week, once I got there, I had to practically turn around and drive back because of work the next day. Most of the time I was alone on the long drive home and the darkness shrouded the road and my soul. Nothing but me and a thousand stars that weren't pointing in any particular direction. I would wonder whether God was listening to my prayers or just ignoring me.

The lady in the bed next to Betty died, and I worried that Betty would be next. But my prayers apparently paid off: thirty days later the doctor discharged her. On the way home that day, I made the point of putting my arm around her and holding her close. Days with her seemed limited in number.

She recovered at her parents' house that winter. While living there, we decided it would work out better for her if she could work part-time at home rather than risk her health traveling to a job. Her illness was a blessing, but one very much disguised at the time. The idea of starting our own small business was born out of her physical adversity. We looked into many business opportunities, including an appliance store, a motel, a packaged sandwich route that a St. Paul sandwich firm talked me out of because Mankato didn't seem big enough to them, and a diaper service that a Chicago diaper service talked me out of for the same reason.

A U.S. Chamber of Commerce booklet was printed for returning servicemen who wanted to start their own small business but were short on ideas. One of its suggestions was a letter service. Copiers didn't exist. So we started a letter service with a castoff mimeograph from the church. It began part-time for Betty at home, but grew quickly. We began March 1948 with $300 and called it Carlson Letter Service. Flyers advertising the service were mailed to fifty businesses in Mankato. First month gross sales were $25, but were growing rapidly. A few months later I added a hobby printing press that came with ten drawers of type and an instruction booklet.

In July a friend from church, Myrtle Swan, asked if I could print wedding invitations for her daughter, La Jean. I had just one type style suitable: Old English. A few weeks later, I approached Brett's Department Store in Mankato with the idea of being a printed napkins dealer. It was an idea I'd borrowed from *Graphic Arts Monthly*. By selling wholesale rather than retail we could expand quickly, plus it was much easier for me to deliver to one location than many. I had to pick up orders and deliver during lunch hour and after work at Swanson's.

My dad said I had "rocks in my head" to start a small business when I had a secure job at Swanson's. I signed up a dozen dealers, all on Saturdays, and left. I've read recently that only one business in five lasts five years. Maybe it was risky, but I had faith in my ability, and in God who would help and guide. It took seven years before our net profits were greater than if I had stayed at Swanson's, and that's figuring in estimated raises. Success didn't happen overnight. I lasted because I'd learned patience in the Army. Slow results didn't bother me. Every spare penny went back into the business.

Up until World War II, weddings were mainly family affairs celebrated at home or in the church parsonage. But after the War, weddings were becoming much larger and being celebrated in churches, thus making printed invitations and napkins a necessity for many brides. It was a good time to start a wedding business.

A daughter, Nancy, was born December 1949, but the joy of her birth was tempered somewhat when the doctor said Betty shouldn't have another child because of her Hodgkin's disease. Because of my growing business commitments, our pastor and his wife, Rev. Charles Duxbury, and Hazel, had to bring Nancy and Betty home from the hospital.

419 Mound Avenue.

Chapter Nine

The 1951 flood was the worst since 1888. Mankato wasn't prepared. Carlson Letter Service was located at our 419 Mound Avenue home where we had lived since early 1947 after Betty's recuperation. It was a small white house with green trim, just two bedrooms, and a basement. The business, which had begun in a bedroom in March 1948, was moved to the basement when we secured the hobby printing press.

We had four hours warning. When the water rose we didn't know what to do at first. Our home and business were in direct danger. Just when we were reaching the point of despair as the rising muddy water was lapping up our lawn, a seed corn plant owner drove his truck down the street and said he had vacant warehouse space where we could store our belongings. His men loaded all our furniture except Betty's piano, which we put on sawhorses.

I worked frantically to save the basement printing presses. Betty, pregnant with our second child, had to leave. A friend carried my 100-pound hobby printing press up the stairs by himself. Our motorized press was too big, so we greased the parts that could rust and left it. I bagged the basement windows with chunks of sod, thinking that would keep the water out. Having never been through a flood, I didn't realize the tremendous pressure water creates against a house foundation. While I was upstairs, the flood water broke through the basement window with a resounding crash. It scared the living daylights out of me and I ran down the steps and out the door. As it turned out, the water that flooded into the basement through the window equalized pressure with the basement walls and may have saved the house.

Still shaking from the crash of the broken window, I went directly to the Duxburys, who helped us keep the business running with only a one-day lapse. We had two part-timers besides Betty: the Duxbury's daughter and Helen Stansfield, whose husband, Lyle, was my close friend of many years. For a whole month we conducted business on the back porch of the parsonage. Betty, Nancy, the Duxburys and their two children, and myself made for quite a crowd. After living with a family for a month you either hate them or they are friends for life. In our case we became lifelong friends. When the flood water was pumped out of our house weeks later, we discovered that our motorized press had survived. Flood water had reached tabletop level in the kitchen. We moved the business into our single stall garage until the weather cooled that fall. In October 1951, our second daughter, Patty, was born. But the Duxburys weren't there to take Betty and Patty home from the hospital this time. They had left Mankato for another church.

At a Mankato City Council meeting that fall a council member said another flood probably wouldn't occur anytime soon because sixty-three years had passed since the last one. (However, the river flooded again the next year, and if not for a dike recently built along the Minnesota River, our business would have been swamped.) At that same Council meeting I was there to get approval to construct a new business building across the alley from our home. Architectural plans had already been drawn. The City Council turned me down because some of my neighbors had petitioned against it. So we changed plans. This setback became another blessing in disguise because our business grew faster than we anticipated and that little building in the alley would not have been sufficient.

In January 1953 we leased what had been an old hotel and put a new name on the sign out front: Carlson Wedding Service. To cut expenses, we tried subletting the rear of the building to two men who sold water softeners, but they disappeared one night owing one month's rent. A few weeks later the FBI was asking me questions about them. I never rented out a building again. We would be at this location six years.

Besides the business, our family was growing too. So I bought a South Front Street home with a dual purpose: move the home to a lot in another area, and, since it was zoned commercial, construct a building on the site after moving the home. We contracted with a mover and filed the necessary permits. The house was much larger than we had anticipated. Moving from South Front to Hazel Street meant negotiating several difficult turns and in order to do it, the movers had to cut down some trees on the city-owned boulevard. This really irritated many nearby homeowners. Like a penguin, our house waddled down Pleasant Street to Hazel on a short trek across town over the Fourth of July weekend. It took three days, and we left town during the move. Newspaper headlines mentioned it. People were angry at the felled trees, which were replaced later, but the replacement trees weren't nearly as tall. As the movers crossed the slough towards our new lot, they had to take down phone and electric lines. One attorney was really angry when he had to go without supper that night because our movers had shut off his electricity.

We constructed our first company-owned building on the lot at 1015 South Front. In November 1958, when we moved in, Carlson Wedding Service had twenty employees.

Glen Taylor, Merlyn Andersen, Jim and Mary Holland.

CHAPTER TEN

I've often been asked how Carlson Wedding Service grew so rapidly. In the '50s we didn't employ a single salesperson, nor did we advertise in any national publications. There were many reasons why we grew.

One reason was direct mail. Using purchased lists starting in 1950, we mailed letters and samples promoting our service to print shops all around the nation. The results were phenomenal. I wrote the cover letters even though I had never had any training in that. Not once did it ever occur to me that by mailing these sales letters other print shops would steal my idea.

Our company culture helped. I tried to turn our business into a family. We were Mankato's first major employer to offer part-timers benefits, with birthdays and vacations off. We were first to hire a great number of students part-time. When some students couldn't work regular hours, we would change our schedules for them. Former employees still comment about our past picnics, bowling and Christmas parties.

I tried to be accepting of employees. In the late '60s many of our male employees had long hair. A friend from church asked me to make his son cut his hair as a requirement for him working at Carlson Wedding Service. I wouldn't do it even though his hair had bothered me. Then one morning my attitude changed when, in my bedroom, I glanced up at Sallman's rendition of Jesus and sensed that if I could worship a God with long hair, perhaps I could live with it in my employees.

I developed periodic employee reviews in which I would hear both constructive and not-so-constructive criticism from employees. An employee could talk with me one-on-one. In the same vein I introduced the exit interview, which improved operations further.

Our line of work helped us succeed. We specialized in a very narrow range of printed products: the wedding field. One of the best business decisions I made was to sell wholesale versus retail. Even though the profit per dollar was less, the number of dealers and sales was unlimited.

Our upper management helped us succeed. A growing business needs capable people who can handle responsibility. My earliest memory of delegating authority was to give some printing responsibility to Merlyn Anderson, when he first started in the '50s. By the summer of 1959, we had grown to twenty-five employees. Betty and I were planning a long overdue vacation, and we needed someone in charge while we were away. Vivian Kent, an office worker, had the most maturity, and was the logical choice after a young man, Menno Fast, turned me down to be our full-time director. The day before we were to leave, I told the staff to send away any college students looking for part-time work. And predictably, that day, a young college student came in and the office staff sent him away. I wandered into the office just as he was walking out the front door. While seeing him go, I had second thoughts. We really needed a part-time employee in the napkin printing department and stockroom. So I hollered down the street. "Hey, come back," I said. "I want to talk." In the interview I learned he had been raised on a farm, and he was married with a child. I figured he would be dependable. He was Glen Taylor. So I marked on his application "hired" and asked him to start Monday. Meanwhile, we left for California the next day. Apparently I'd failed to tell the staff about Glen being hired and they had to search in my office for the application. They assigned him to work.

It was God's handiwork. Just minutes later and Glen Taylor, and Carlson Wedding Service, would have had vastly different futures. I feel our company gave him a better opportunity for success than what he would have had with many other companies. I can't take credit for hiring Glen, or any other employee. God directed, and helped us.

Another "coincidence" that helped us occurred soon thereafter. A friend, Floyd Watts, who would later own a Mankato overhead door business, asked me if I could make use of a $10,000 loan. Apparently Floyd had seen the business grow and believed a loan to us would be a solid investment for him. He said to me: "Bill, in business you either go forward or backward, you seldom stand still." I invested virtually all of the loan money into new dealer catalogs. I had known the importance of a first-rate catalog from receiving the Mankato Commercial College piece in the '30s, but had never had the money to really do it right at Carlson Wedding Service. Now I could. In 1960, with a competitive catalog, sales rose 49 percent. It was the best year in company history. The $10,000 printed 1,000 new catalogs. For the first time our catalog quality matched that of our largest competitors.

An important reason we succeeded was our organization. We incorporated in 1962 as Carlson Wedding Service about the same time we moved from Mankato to a larger building at 100 Garfield in North Mankato. I'd read enough business articles to realize that a corporation was the safest way to provide benefits for a growing business. At commercial college, I'd taken a business law course and only one idea stuck in my mind from it: "A partnership is a poor ship to sail in." A sole proprietorship could be even riskier.

I called my three key people "supervisors" and delegated direct responsibility to them: Jim Holland headed the office, Merlyn Anderson, printing, and Glen Taylor, napkins and purchasing. Two-thirds of our sixty employees in 1962 were college students, and I couldn't supervise all of them. Below Merlyn, Glen and Jim, we hired college students as part-time supervisors as well, and several of them became full-time as the business grew. By hiring part-timers, we could watch their work ethic without investing too much in them. If they worked out, we offered them full-time jobs upon their graduation.

Unlike Merlyn and Glen, Jim Holland hadn't grown up on a farm, nor had he risen through the company ranks. At my retirement, Jim was the only manager not promoted from within. I had known of him through his wife, Mary, who worked in our office. He had the talents I needed in an office manager. After his graduation, Jim taught school in Wisconsin, where I sought him out and persuaded him to come work for us. When the three were named VPs in 1966, at the suggestion of Ed McLean, my attorney, I paid Jim a little less than Merlyn and Glen based on seniority. Ed believed the new titles would be good for the three psychologically. Their pay stayed the same and so did their responsibilities.

We grew because of wise counsel. In the late '60s, while reading *Graphic Arts Monthly* again, I discovered SCORE, a national organization of retired executives. These people donate their time and talent to help business owners who can't afford professional business advice. I met with a SCORE counselor three times. He had started and sold three different businesses and seemed highly competent. He said we'd become complacent because business had been too good, and he suggested a better table of organization that placed one person in charge in case I became ill or died. Having three men on equal footing wasn't right. Even though I'd missed only a few days due to illness since 1948, I realized I couldn't work fifty to seventy hour weeks indefinitely without becoming sick. After the consultation, I asked him to put his opinions in writing. Soon thereafter I chose Glen to be over the other two as an executive vice president. On a scale of one to five, with five being most competitive, I'd give Glen a five. A company leader must be competitive or the business won't survive. Naturally, I worried how Jim and Merlyn would react, but they graciously accepted my decision, and understood the SCORE representative's advice.

With that reasoning, in 1967, I developed a buy-sell agreement to clarify the succession of power. I'd gleaned the idea from a business magazine article that said every company needed a systematic succession plan. The agreement allowed Merlyn, Jim and Glen first crack at buying Carlson Wedding Service, and in it I promised to retire no later than my sixty-third birthday. Betty wasn't in favor of it, and she let me know it. She'd wanted us to hand the business over to a son-in-law. Neil, who had married my older daughter Nancy, was a Christian and had worked part-time at Carlson Craft, but he wasn't old enough to take over. Years later he became a pastor, and was very successful in that field. Patty's husband had never worked at Carlson Craft. With the agreement, my vice presidents had a future and incentive to stay. I'm convinced that if I hadn't developed the agreement, with their age and ingenuity, one or all of them could have started their own competing business in time.

Like my decision to bring in a SCORE counselor, I made many other business decisions over lunch while reading business magazines at the Happy Chef Restaurant in North Mankato. I read magazines there nearly every day, usually by myself, something which helped make up for my lack of formal education. It also helped me get away from office pressures. I always read *Graphic Arts Monthly*, *Nation's Business*, and *Business Week*.

One mark of our success was my attitude towards debt. The only money I ever borrowed was from the Bank of Commerce, and the most owed was $90,000 at any one time. We limited growth to available funds. When I grew up it was wise to avoid debt, and that experience carried over to my business. My dad continually warned me about debt because he had lost his farm that way. The only personal debt I've had was a house mortgage. I avoid risk. People have lost farms and homes when they've had too much debt in property. I've cautioned my daughters and grandchildren about it. When I bought my first car in December 1938, Minnesota law allowed up to 36 percent interest on small loans. Being young and stupid, I bought the car anyway. Even now I hate it when I forget to pay credit card bills on time and get socked with interest. It's money down the drain.

Many businesses fail because the owner drinks too much. I've never, in all my life, been drunk. While working for a farmer during the mid-'30s, right after Prohibition lifted, I did drink a homemade brew of sorts and took a liking to it for a few weeks. But I had learned enough from the Methodist Church to know that what I was doing was a bad habit, if not immoral. So I quit.

One last personal trait that helped me succeed was the perseverance I learned through trials. I graduated from high school during the Depression, and had to wait four years before I could afford commercial college. So I made the best of it. In the Army I served fifty-six months when I initially thought I'd be out in twelve. I had to make the best of that. In business it took seven years before I made more profit than if I'd stayed with Swanson's. In marriage, I suffered right along with Betty through her many illnesses. God has taught me through experience to persevere and have faith when times go awry. Learned perseverance has been the factor most vital to my personal and business success. My favorite scripture verse has always been Philippians 4:13: "I can do all things through Christ Who gives me strength."

Our first motorized press.

CHAPTER ELEVEN

I learned quite early on that it's just as important to buy right as to sell right. For example, in 1949, our overhead was such that we could offer dealers a forty-five percent trade discount on wholesale wedding invitations. Most of our competitors were offering fifty percent. When I switched suppliers in the mid-'50s, I could buy at a better price, which enabled us to offer a fifty percent trade discount. It helped secure more dealers.

In the early '50s I was buying ninety-five percent of our blank stock from William House, a New York City firm which Glen Taylor now owns. One day in 1955, a visitor knocked at my door, one Palmer Gilbertson, a former editor of the *Lake Crystal Tribune*. He owned Mission Announcement Company of San Gabriel, California, which was a business similar to ours, and he had just arrived from New York City. Most paper merchants in New York were Jewish in those days. So Palmer said to me: "Let's pool our purchases to see if a couple of Swedes can do business with the Jewish paper merchants." By combining orders we could buy at a better price from Brooklyn Announcement, he said. His shipments would go through the Panama Canal to San Diego, and mine would go by rail to Mankato. He laid the groundwork. Brooklyn Announcement and William House were fierce competitors. After buying from Brooklyn Announcement with Palmer's help, a William House VP visited Mankato to learn why our orders with them had fallen off drastically. Of course, William House lowered its prices. Consequently, we could offer dealers a fifty percent trade discount on all wedding invitations.

Ink came from a Minneapolis wholesaler, Perfection Type, who also sold Virkotypes, a baking oven that produced thermography-type raised lettering. When we expanded we added more of their machines because brides liked the look and feel of the printing. We stressed speed because brides often worked on tight timetables, but quality was just as crucial. Our inspectors had to catch any misprints before they went out the door. A dealer in Florida had been buying from a competitor of ours in Atlanta, but they discovered they could receive better and more reliable service from us in Mankato after sending orders via Air Mail.

We identified competitors from trade journals, and compared

their catalogs with ours to see if they had a special design. Another move was to begin using the name "Carlson Craft" in the late '60s. Now it's a registered name with the U.S. Office of Patents and Copyrights. No one else can use that name or emblem.

The number of dealers behind on overdue invoices was extremely low. Each year we set aside 15/100ths of one percent of sales as bad debt reserve. In 1973, the IRS fined us $900 because they said our reserve had been too large. They said we should have taken the previous five years of bad debt and used that for future reserves instead of 15/100ths. Since I had lived through the Great Depression, I knew the economy could fluctuate considerably and that it may not do it within every five-year window. I proved the IRS wrong. The next year we wiped out the entire reserve during the '74 recession. And even though they were wrong, the IRS still kept our $900. I should have asked for it back!

The only time we faced litigation was when we were trying to expand our North Mankato building across the alley and into vacant land. We tried to buy it. But local residents, who had used the property as a gardens, blocked us. It turned out to be yet another blessing in disguise. We later purchased ten acres on the North Mankato hilltop and, at the urging of my vice presidents, built a warehouse there.

At one point we thought about going public. Public companies can generate extra funds by selling stock. It's usually easier than borrowing. But we didn't need extra funds for growth. We also had two chances to sell out. Glen Taylor eventually bought both of the companies that made us an offer. In both cases, as a management team, we realized at least one of us would have to leave Mankato with a buyout. None of us wanted to move. Besides, we didn't have to sell.

I frequently compared our hourly workers' pay with the average U.S. hourly wage rate as stated in the *Wall Street Journal*. Our wages were lower because we were outstate and had a high number of part-time employees. The ratio we created from the *Wall Street Journal* numbers and our wage rates gave us a year-to-year handle on pay. Another ratio determined my pay and that of the VPs. In my last years, when Glen was executive vice president, his pay was just below mine, and the others slightly below Glen's. A ten percent gap separated my pay from that of Jim Holland's.

My family.

CHAPTER TWELVE

Betty took notes on her medical problems and in recent years I found some of them. In one note she said she couldn't have made it physically nearly as many years if it hadn't been for me. I tried to listen, talk and understand her. I would put myself in her shoes, and try to figure out why she felt the way she did. A former pastor of ours believed Betty was taking out her resentment of her physical problems on me because I was the one closest to her.

She was very outgoing, organized, had many friends, and would speak her mind. Conversely, I was reserved and wouldn't make public statements. When she thought, it passed through her lips. At times she acted on emotion. She never argued in larger groups where it might embarrass someone, but more in smaller groups or one-on-one. She had a high school education and was a good typist. During the War she had worked for the draft board and had to endure many emotional moments when parents were saying their good-byes to sons leaving for war.

We didn't have a family prayer time, something I regret. Many times early on in our marriage I wanted a special place in the house where we could pray together, but there really wasn't a suitable place to do it. Business had taken up all the free space. Falling into that pattern set a precedent for later years when we didn't pray much as husband and wife, except for table grace. We did attend church regularly and prayed there.

She worked hard in the early years of the business, and was a great helper. The first seven years when we weren't making much profit, she would often encourage me during periods of doubt. It was a team effort at the beginning. She did all the book work through 1954 before staying home with Nancy and Patty. After Patty left home in 1972, Betty worked part-time at Carlson Craft just to offset the "empty nest" syndrome.

One decision that affected me most was retiring three years earlier than planned. Even though I had pledged to retire at sixty-three in my buy-sell agreement, I ended up retiring at fifty-nine in December 1974. Had I worked those extra three years I probably would have gained much in wealth. The firm was beginning to take off, but at that time I didn't know how many years Betty would live. In a public speech near retirement, I stated that "there are more important things in life than building up a big bank account."

She had Hodgkin's disease in 1948, and a recurrence five years later. In 1972, she had breast cancer, and lost one breast. Skin cancer afflicted her three times. In 1979 she was diagnosed with disseminated histoplasmosis. It was a fungus that traveled into her liver, bone marrow and lung. It had a very high mortality rate. It's acquired through the dust and droppings of birds. We think Betty picked it up in North Mankato near Spring Lake where ducks gather and leave droppings. Betty then was stricken with colon cancer, and passed away January 1988.

Had I known then what I know now, I still wouldn't have traded those three years for the surety of becoming independently wealthy. A dollar price can't be put on time with a spouse. We produced a lot of things at Carlson Craft, but we never could figure out how to produce Time. In spite of her illnesses, Betty and I had two daughters. Nancy bore three children: Jeffrey, Betsy and Jonathan. Patty also had three children: Benjamin, Rachel and Andrew. My six grandchildren and one great-grandchild, Micah, all have brought a special joy to my life.

Brad Schreier.

Chapter Thirteen

A few articles published on Glen's meteoric rise have disappointed me because I felt they gave little credit to my era. Then in 1998, at Carlson Craft's fiftieth anniversary, much of that feeling of neglect faded away when the company emphasized the early years. Granted, the company grew dramatically after 1975, but it also grew dramatically before 1975 as well – we had started from zero. At my retirement Carlson Craft was the nation's third-largest wedding wholesaler. A few years later it was the largest.

After the fiftieth celebration, Brad Schreier, current president of Taylor Corporation, mentioned in a newsletter how thankful they were that I had sold the business on a very fair basis. I didn't take advantage of them. I sold Carlson Wedding Service to three men on a promissory note 1 1/2 percent lower than what our bank would have charged. In a strict business sense, it didn't make sense. If Glen had "gone under" I would have gone under with him. Nearly all my investments were tied up in Carlson Craft. Yet I trusted them. The start I gave them was a factor in the company's later success.

My attorney, Ed McLean, had worked with a number of buy-sell agreements before, but ours, he said, had been extremely liberal on the part of the seller. I made it easy for them to buy because that's my nature. I cared for Glen, Merlyn and Jim, and wished them well. Perhaps I gave away more than most rational men would, but I will never regret it. In 1962, Ed had suggested that I personally own the company buildings, and separate them out from the corporation. I eventually followed his advice. So just before I retired, I began leasing the main building to Carlson Craft. After I sold out, they continued renting. The rental rate mirrored the Bureau of Labor Statistics Cost of Living Index. If at year's end inflation had risen four percent, then Carlson Craft's rent would rise four percent. This built-in safeguard was my family's only inflation hedge since the last dollars paid to me in the buy-out, in 1984, would certainly be watered down by inflation. Those dollars were worth about fifty cents compared with the 1974 dollars. I'd been warned by a Mankato business owner, who had been stuck in a lease without inflation protection, not to sign one without it. The lease was supposed to run eight years, but I reluctantly sold the building in 1978 at book value plus ten percent to Glen, who wanted to buy it.

Glen ran his own show after I left. One early decision was to take a price increase that eventually made him much more profit in 1975 than I had made in 1974. Perhaps I had been too concerned about market share, sales volume and signing on new dealers, and not paying as much attention to generating profit for expansion. Within two years, Glen had catapulted Carlson Craft forward as the largest wedding wholesaler in the country.

He and I had been heading in different directions. I was looking forward to spending less time at work; he was just the opposite. I'd made my fortune, and he was wanting to make his. He was looking to expand; I was tapering off. It boggles my mind, according to some published estimates, how well Glen has done for himself financially. His name appears in national magazines on high net worth lists. I wish him well, but I don't envy him. He's had a heart attack, and I'm thankful that I have never had to live with his pressures.

The Book of Golden Deeds Award.

Chapter Fourteen

Yes, there is life after Carlson Craft.

Even though tithing is an Old Testament principle, I still feel it's important because it acknowledges God as the source of our resources. I feel ten percent should be the minimum to give back to Him. I tried to apply the tithing concept in business. In the early '70s, I read in the *Wall Street Journal* where Dayton Corporation sent five percent of its net profits to charity, which was the maximum allowed by law. So we started a similar program at Carlson Craft, and by 1975 were giving away three percent of net. I know today Carlson Craft gives liberally, and I hope they've achieved five percent.

Some people tithe ten percent of gross, while others tithe ten percent after tax. I tithe off gross. Since I started it in 1960, I think the extra money I've donated to charitable organizations has been money well spent. I have gained more than I have lost. After retirement I made some large contributions to my national church after receiving money from the sale of the business. In 1977, Betty and I also made a major gift to our local church.

The IRS has audited me twice since retirement. Both times they said I was giving away too much money, by their standards, to charity. Even though I said I had canceled checks to prove my donations, both times they had to send an auditor to my house to see for themselves. The second time they sent a young woman fresh from college who seemed very efficient, and in looking over my canceled checks discovered I'd missed one $30 donation. So I should have paid even less tax.

I worked on my national Disciples of Christ board for eight years, and on its regional board for eight. Our local church has wavered through the years between the Disciples of Christ and the Church of Christ. Herman Kooy, who was a Church of Christ pastor, served until 1941. A Disciples of Christ minister served until 1954, after which a Church of Christ pastor came on. Since then it's been all Disciples of Christ. In my local church I've served on most boards and committees, including board chairman, elder, deacon, Sunday School teacher, and Sunday School superintendent. Currently I'm church historian and serve on the membership/evangelism committee. I thoroughly enjoyed teaching Sunday School from 1958 to 1962. Those twelve-year-olds were eager to learn and I tried pointing them in the right direction. Years later, a person from that class told me their life had been challenged in various ways towards the right because of it. Beverley Duxbury, my first employee, once said: "Whenever I do a job more efficiently, I always think of Bill and the good work habits he instilled in me."

Besides church, I've been involved with a number of nonprofits. Immediately after retirement, I was so caught up helping these nonprofit boards and organizations, nineteen in all, that I had to make a detailed chart to avoid meeting conflicts. One can't be very effective when "watered down," so I gradually reduced my commitments considerably down to my two favorite charities: MRCI and Courage Center. MRCI helps good people with a physical or mental limitation by providing them a home and work experience. I was board president for one year and on the committee that helped build the recent facility.

When I started with Courage Center it was called the Minnesota Society for Crippled Children and Adults. I was on its board for twelve years. At my last meeting, I figured I had driven over 25,000 miles to attend its various meetings and camps over the years. It serves people with physical, not mental, impairments. Camp Courage, which is part of Courage Center and located near Maple Lake, accepts physically handicapped teenagers. Campers meet peers with similar experiences. Another camp serves young cancer patients as well. Courage North, where I was camping committee building chairman, accepts hearing impaired kids. One time at Camp Courage, I especially remember a particular wheelchair-bound young man who seemed so happy. You wouldn't think he had a care in the world. Courage Center had been the highlight of his year.

Courage Center's headquarters is in Golden Valley, Minnesota, and that site has various physical rehabilitation programs, including pool therapy. An annex building houses paralyzed youth. Dedicated instructors receive people with rehabilitation potential from a home situation where the parents may not be able to help. The instructors help them live with others in a group home. Some of these people are quadriplegics. I learned of Courage Center while on the MRCI board. A former Mankato mayor, Rex Hill, who was going off the Courage Center board, heard of my interest in handicapped people and the following week they asked me to serve.

In 1980, I was nominated for the Minnesota Business Hall of Fame, and even though someone else received top place, it was an honor to be nominated. In 1982, the local Sertoma Club awarded me, along with Vivian Jensen, its Service to Mankind Award. I was a WCCO Good Neighbor Award winner in 1985, which was the same year the Mankato Exchange Club presented me with the award I cherish most: the Book of Golden Deeds Award. The local paper's headline read: "Carlson a Job Giver to Thousands of Students."

Trains have been my main hobby, and I really enjoy riding them. Train rides have come at significant times in my life. The Durango-Silverton narrow gauge in southwestern Colorado uses a steam engine that reminds me of the one on my first trip to Mankato. I've taken the Orient Express and the Swiss Alpine Express, which is one of the most beautiful train trips in the whole world. Model railroading intrigues me, as does watercolor and oil painting. I took painting classes so I would have something to do after retirement. If practiced more, I think I could be fairly good at it. One of my paintings hangs at Taylor Corporation headquarters. Glen once stated that it was part of his presentation of southern Minnesota artists, which is flattering, but I hardly consider myself a real artist.

Since trains don't run across the ocean I flew to Sweden in 1977. I wanted to visit my ancestral village but couldn't with the large tour group. Just to be in the country felt exhilarating.

Me and Glen Taylor in 1988.

Chapter Fifteen

The feeling that Carlson Craft used to be mine has faded over the years. The fiftieth anniversary experience in 1998 brought that feeling back for a moment. I thought the company would limit its recognition of the fiftieth to a float in the North Mankato Centennial parade, but they went far beyond that. With attendance over 6,000, it was the biggest event in Mankato history by any one firm. I was honored and humbled at the huge celebration. I shook hands again with people I'd worked alongside. I'm very proud of Brad Schreier, president of Taylor Corp., a very good man who shares my Christian beliefs. Brad was hired by Glen in 1970. He started as a part-time college student, became a supervisor, and was hired full-time after graduation. Employees can sense when a boss is genuine, and Brad is genuine. He and Staff Harder, president of Carlson Craft, have continued some of the same business principles we started when I was there. Staff also practices his Christian beliefs.

Brad sent me this message once, and it still means a lot: "Again I want to thank you for planting the seed and providing for a solid foundation for Carlson Craft and the Taylor Corporation. Without this solid foundation we would not be where we are today. Many, many people have contributed to this success. But without your vision and entrepreneurial spirit those collective dreams of Carlson Craft would not have been significantly realized."

Glen has also acknowledged his thanks to me in a letter. On May 8, 1998, he wrote: "I want to share with you how much I have enjoyed reading the three-part articles in the newsletter for Carlson Craft employees where you wrote about the history of your business. On receipt of the *Connect Business Magazine*, I noted the interesting article where they had interviewed you.

"They are both very nice articles and I appreciate your willingness to share with others your belief and experiences.

"Even though I have heard most of these stories many times, it is still refreshing and emotional for me to hear your version of the story again. On numerous occasions I have shared with others areas in which you have mentored me. Those learning experiences in which I have gained from you have helped me in my dealings with people and with future growth.

"Each time that I meet with employees, I begin by thanking them for their contribution and conclude with a 'thank you' for what we expect of them to accomplish in the future. Though I have thanked you, I am sure that I could not possibly express to you adequately for the opportunities, love and guidance that you gave me for many years. I have been blessed as you mentioned in the article to have worked with people that I cared about, respect and thoroughly enjoyed – my very best friends. In conclusion, thank you. I wish you and your loved ones the very best.

"One of your students, Glen Taylor."

Me and Vi ~ again.

CHAPTER SIXTEEN

When Betty died in January 1988 I was stricken, but it was ten weeks later when I really bottomed out. A visit with friends helped me cope after I cried on their shoulder. Yes, I believed in life after death and expected to see Betty in heaven, but I still missed her. With two daughters and six grandchildren though, I wasn't totally alone in the world.

The first Saturday of May 1988, I drove to Slayton, Minnesota, with the stated intent to visit two cousins, but I really went there to see Vi. She had married Willard Lundblad, a Slayton farmer, in 1948, and had had a good marriage with him, and raised two sons before he died in 1978 from cancer. Vi had taught school for thirty-three years. It was almost fifty years to the day after we started going steady in 1938. My older daughter, Nancy, was apprehensive and felt seeing Vi just five months after Betty's death might be inappropriate or even risky. Patty went along with it. Had I not known Vi before it would have been too soon to start dating.

Four weeks after seeing each other, we decided to marry. Vi's sister, Muriel, recognized me right away even though she'd been only eleven in 1940. She approved of our marriage. Her two sons gave the okay. Our love was relit and we knew it could continue.

Then on June 6, 1988, in the basement bathroom of my home, I took hold of my wedding ring, the ring that had symbolized my relationship with Betty, and tried to slip it off my finger. Vi wasn't wearing hers because Willard had died ten years before. Should I take mine off too? I couldn't get it over my knuckle. I tried soap and water and finally it loosened a bit. So I reached down to take it off, but something kept holding me back. I couldn't budge it – not because I couldn't physically take it off, but because I felt I would be abandoning Betty if I did. We had been married over forty years. Thoughts of her flooded my mind and I began praying out loud. Suddenly an audible voice came over my right shoulder and said: "Now is the time, my son." I've heard people who claim they've heard a voice from God, but I never thought it would happen to me. I took the ring off. God had spoken.

I gave Vi a dime store engagement ring in July 1988, and a real one soon thereafter. She tried to explain how upset she had been after her mother had made her break off her relationship with me.

That summer we planned a wedding for the next spring, but after talking to her pastor, and in our own minds, we thought, Why wait? We married October 15, 1988, and have been very happy since. She loves my family, and I love hers. The secret to our marriage is prayer. Her parents prayed together each day, and we do the same.

Thank God For Today

This is the beginning of a new day.

I can waste it or use it for good.

What I do today is important because I am exchanging a day of my life for it.

When tomorrow comes, this day will be gone forever ~ leaving in its place something I have traded for it.

I want it to be gain, not loss; good, not evil; success, not failure; in order that I shall not regret the price I have paid for today.

~Anonymous

In memory of Betty H. Carlson
1920~1988